SECRETS TO SUCCESS

*The Definitive Career Development Guide for
New and First Generation Professionals*

by

AL COLEMAN, JR.

TELEMACHUS
PRESS

Secrets to Success: The Definitive Career Development Guide for New and First Generation Professionals

THIS BOOK IS BASED SOLELY ON THE AUTHOR'S EXPERIENCE AND OPINION AND IS OF GENERAL APPLICATION. THE INFORMATION CONTAINED WITHIN IS NOT INTENDED TO BE ADVICE SPECIFIC TO YOUR SITUATION. BECAUSE YOUR SITUATION MAY BE DIFFERENT, PLEASE CONSULT WITH YOUR APPLICABLE PROFESSIONAL ADVISOR BEFORE USING ANY OF THE ENCLOSED INFORMATION, IDEAS OR PRACTICES.

The publisher does not have any control over and does not assume any responsibility for author or third-party websites or their content.

Cover designed by Telemachus Press, LLC

Cover art:
Copyright © iStockPhoto #2158778

Author photo credit Khary D. Hornsby www.kdiarra.com

Published by Telemachus Press, LLC
http://www.telemachuspress.com

Visit the author's website at
http://www.alcolemanjr.com

ISBN# 978-1-937387-48-8 (eBook)
ISBN# 978-1-937387-49-5 (paperback)

Library of Congress Control Number: 2011939363

Version 20110.09.21

Printed in the United States of America
10 9 8 7 6 5 4 3 2 1

DEDICATIONS

Thank you Lord for providing me with the knowledge, wisdom and strength to share these truths with the world.

To my wife, I love you; thank you for allowing me to share my time, talent and treasure with others. To my children, you continue to be my inspiration. To my family and friends, thank you for your encouragement and support. To my City—Midway, Central & Grotto—*We did it.*

In loving memory of Alfred W. Coleman, III

Funded by
MISSION COLLEGE
Carl D. Perkins Vocational and Technical Education Act Grant

SECRETS TO SUCCESS

*The Definitive Career Development Guide for
New and First Generation Professionals*

*Required reading for any young or first generation professional
that wants personal, professional and financial success, without
sacrificing who you are or what you care about.*

SUMMARY

Secrets to Success: The Definitive Career Development Guide for New and First Generation Professionals is required reading for any young or first generation professional in the field of law, medicine, education, business, government, non-profit, engineering, science, technology, media or mass communications, art or design, entertainment, or any of the life, physical, or social sciences.

It provides detailed guidance on how to become personally, professionally and financially successful, without sacrificing who you are and what you care about. Designed for tomorrow's leaders, it candidly emphasizes that nothing in life is new; and acknowledges that even though you can gain wisdom from your mistakes, it's easier and less costly to learn from the mistakes of others.

In about the same time it takes to watch a movie, you'll learn principles rarely taught to new and first generation professionals; including how to avoid losing up to $80,000 per year by graduating on time from college or a graduate program, with minimal student-loan debt. You'll discover how to find a mentor and increase your income by up to $22,000 by doing so. And explore how to find the job of your dreams, keep it for a lifetime—if you want, and effortlessly create wealth now and for future generations. You'll uncover all of this and more while learning how to stay healthy, happy and stress-free during the entire process.

TABLE OF CONTENTS

PROLOGUE
MONDAY, OCTOBER 19TH, 2009

Monday, October 19th, 2009.

I don't remember much about that day. I don't remember what I wore. I don't remember what I ate. I don't remember my conversations throughout the day. I don't remember what I did at work. All I remember is that it was Monday. I remember because I teach on Mondays.

I remember going to class and having fun with my students, and having a great class. Everything was perfect, except for the constant vibration of my phone. It rang so much that I had to take it out of my pocket during the middle of class and set it on the table in front of me, underneath the small podium, before continuing to teach.

I taught two classes that Monday; that I remember. I remember going to my second class, and lecturing like I always did. Nothing was out of the ordinary. When class ended at 7:25 pm I walked from the University buildings through the skyway tunnel to the parking garage. Along the way it dawned on me that I had messages on my phone

i

from earlier. I pulled my phone out and saw the home screen cluttered with several missed calls, most of which were from my sister.

I decided to call her back first. I knew that if something had happened, she would give me the news without hesitation. I dialed her number and nervously awaited the voice on the other end. She picked up after several rings, as if she was preparing herself for the ensuing conversation. "Hello?" she said, and immediately started crying as she recognized my voice.

I don't remember the words exchanged over the next twenty minutes we stayed on the phone, but I do remember these two words:

Dad's Dead.

Those two words are the reason you're reading this book.

Dad's Dead.

Those two words motivated me to do what I thought was impossible.

Dad's Dead.

Those two words are the reason I want to share everything I've learned with you about personal, professional and financial success.

UNFINISHED BUSINESS

My dad died at 54 years old. And even though 54 is relatively early to leave this earth, he lived a full life with few regrets. He traveled, saw the world, started and led numerous businesses, and even served in several high-profile government positions in his native country of Liberia.

His untimely demise was foreshadowed by years of illness that plagued him. He had several extended stays in hospitals throughout his final years; with some visits seeming like the end was imminent. However, he would somehow find a way to make it through. During this process I came to accept that his death would inevitably come. And through that acceptance I began attempting to preserve all of the information I could about this well-read, well-traveled, captain of industry. I was determined to ensure that all of the knowledge gained from his 54 years of life would not go to waste.

I spent many Saturday mornings visiting with him, with my son close at hand. We'd participate in his favorite pastime, commenting on cable news shows, during which I'd pepper him with questions to probe his thoughts on various issues.

A few weeks prior to his passing, I kept our weekly appointment and stopped by earlier than usual to check on him. As I walked up the stairs to his bedroom, I saw him shuffling back and forth, with my cousin Doug beside him carrying a large desktop computer in hand. My dad, as I would soon discover, was turning the guest bedroom into an office. The act itself wasn't that odd given the many projects he started once his illness worsened. I was more puzzled by the fact that he was taking on this project given his recent return from a prolonged hospital stay. A stay that seemed to include many more tubes and monitors than recent visits.

I slowed him down just enough to ask what he intended to do in his new digs. He enthusiastically responded, "I'm writing a book." Confused, I inquired; "about what?" He quipped "about my life." I quickly disregarded his comment as another attempt to keep his mind off the recent disappointment that his health wasn't improving.

Several weeks passed and we didn't speak about his book again until he was rushed to the hospital for the final time. During one of our many bedside chats I found the courage to ask him about his last wishes. He was noticeably reluctant to approach this topic and spent the first few minutes rambling through what seemed like random thoughts. Slowly, as the inevitability of his mortality revealed the truth that we both knew, but certainly wouldn't admit; he revealed to me that anything I wanted to know would be found in a briefcase, in his bedroom closet. "Look in the briefcase after I'm gone," he said, "I've written everything down for you and your siblings, everything you need to know is in the briefcase."

Although the grief that would shortly follow was too much to bear, I was comforted by the fact that his legacy would live on through his final testament. To be honest, I was surprised that he followed through. I couldn't believe he did it. My dad had done many extraordinary things in his life, and this certainly ranked at the top. I was amazed that he had the strength during what he may have known to be his final months, to share his final thoughts with us.

THE BRIEFCASE

As I drove to his home the evening of his death, I found an odd sense of calm knowing whatever answers he didn't have a chance to provide due to his illness, would likely be addressed in his "book." After saying my final goodbye and handling the formalities with the coroner, I relayed my father's instructions and disclosed the location of the briefcase to my stepmother and younger siblings. Once the few family and friends who stopped by to offer their condolences left for the evening, we quickly rushed upstairs to find and open the briefcase.

As we approached his bedroom thoughts rushed through my head, "what will it say?" "What did he want us to know?" Each step brought a new question racing through my brain. We entered the room and opened the closet. On the floor, tucked beneath his clothes just as he described was a brown, worn out suitcase that looked as though it had seen its fair share of cities. The front of the case had a gold plated lock with scores of nicks and scratches. I knew immediately my father's travel companion would prove to be a worthy foe.

Realizing that I came horribly prepared to do battle with the keeper of secrets, I yelled for my younger brother to bring up a screwdriver. No lock was going to keep me from seeing the desires of my father's heart on this night. Within seconds the screwdriver was thrust into my hands. I took it firmly and pushed it through the gap between the lock and the briefcase. With an empowering mix of anger and adrenaline; I lifted as hard as I could, slicing the inner half of my palm as I guided the handle upwards, and heard the lock snap and succumb to my force.

The room was dead silent. We huddled around the case as I moved it to the bed and slowly began removing the contents like a veteran curator of precious artifacts. With each item sprawled across the bed, my sister's words returned to me.

Dad's Dead.

I promptly scanned the contents.

Dad's Dead.

Titles to land. Family photos. Business correspondence.

Dad's Dead.

A glimpse into the mind of the man who was never to return began to emerge before my eyes.

Dad's Dead.

His letter's requesting financing for various business deals, post cards from past trips. Personal notes from business acquaintances.

Dad's Dead.

It was voyeuristic; we were viewing things that had been locked away, things that were kept from our view for over twenty years—with one glaring omission. My heart sunk.

Dad's Dead.

Where is it, I began lifting the documents one by one.

Dad's Dead.

My chest was pounding. He couldn't have, he wouldn't have.

Dad's Dead.

I yelled to my brother to look in the closet to make sure there wasn't another briefcase, but I already knew. This was it.

Dad's Dead.

The puzzled look on their faces told me that they knew as well.

Dad's Dead.

It wasn't here. The book. It wasn't in the briefcase.

"Look closer" my sister nervously shouted, "is it under any of the letters?" None of the items could be confused for it. You couldn't fit 54 years into a one-page letter. You couldn't share the wisdom of five decades on the back of a postcard. There's no way a photo could capture the wisdom of a life lived over half a century.

Dad's Dead.

The finality of what had occurred, or more importantly what hadn't, finally sunk in. We all slowly began to accept it. Dad was dead. And whether due to health, fatigue, or the grandeur of capturing your thoughts, wisdom, hopes, wishes and dreams—we had nothing, no words, no teachings, no life lesson, and no diary to satisfy our need to know how he did it. How did he rise from humble beginnings to a position of power and authority, respected by many? How did he lose it all during a brutal civil war that gripped his West African homeland, only to regroup and re-launch himself on the path to success?

I may have been willing to brush it off. To discount the need to have such answers. But any thought of moving on without closure was shattered when I witnessed the 500-person tribute at his funeral. Scores of individuals from all parts of the globe made the journey to our humble mid-western city in the chill of autumn to pay their respects to this man. A man who I admittedly knew better as a friend than as a father due to a divorce that separated us physically and emotionally during my formative years. I had to know. I had to understand. How did this man, a man that I had come to admire, achieve such great success in his life?

As I began preparing to deliver his eulogy, I started to learn more about my father as well as my grandfather, whom I never knew, and was startled by themes in their lives that paralleled my life as well. It was a weird sense of familiarity with the unfamiliar. I began to gain a clearer understanding of his drive, motivation and ambition.

The more I learned the more the tragedy of my loss began to loom over me. For all of my father's greatness, he never truly had an opportunity to share his secrets, the formula to his success; what he did, how he did it and why he did it. His primary method of teaching and grooming me for the challenges that life would present involved admitting his failures to me.

Instead of telling me what worked, he'd usually spend time focusing on what didn't work, to ensure that even if I didn't know with certainty how to achieve success, I would surely know what not to do. I thanked him for this a few months prior to his death. My gratitude was expressed for what I called his "perfect imperfections"— his ability to teach me what to do, by sharing what not to do.

As I shared with him how much I appreciated his candor and humility shown over the years by making himself vulnerable through these unguarded moments; he calmly wiped tears from his eyes, never allowing them to fully run down his sunken cheeks.

It was one of the few times I ever saw him cry. No skin biopsy or multiple pokes of a needle or even the prognosis of imminent death could do what those words did. I believe at that moment he knew that he had succeeded as a father. Through the wisdom shared from his failed endeavors, he could rest assured that I had a path to follow. Not the one he would chart for me, but just as important, a path clearly marked by the boundaries of avoidable mistakes.

My father taught me many lessons during his life that I cherish and carry with me today. But most importantly it was his final lesson in death that I employ in all that I do: *ensure that the words and thoughts you hold dear survive you in death, and are utilized by future generations.*

As I sat on the one year anniversary of his death. I began thinking about what legacy I would leave for my three children should I face the same untimely departure. What would I want them to know? What lessons did I want to share? My upbringing with immigrant parents led to me responding to these questions from the perspective of a first generation professional. And in doing so, I've finished what my father intended by leaving my thoughts for future generations.

The information that follows isn't typically located in a single resource. You don't instinctively know the principles discussed unless you were raised in a professional household and were exposed to such concepts. It's a primer, a gateway to start you down your path to personal, professional and financial success. It's my humble attempt at leaving a legacy for my heirs, through giving the greatest good to the greatest number, as Abraham Lincoln encouraged.

CHAPTER 1: MOST THINGS IN LIFE AREN'T NEW

While it's wise to learn from your mistakes, it's wiser to learn from the mistakes of others

There are several truths about anyone reading this book for the first time. You're a young or first generation professional in the field of law, medicine, education, business, government, non-profit, engineering, science, technology, media or mass communications, art or design, entertainment, or one of the life, physical, or social sciences. You want to be successful personally, professionally and financially; but you're currently struggling with managing your career and your finances, while making time for family, friends and other interests outside of work.

You want it all; but as a new or first generation professional you don't know how get it since no one in your family, and likely none of your friends, have traveled this path. Besides, you don't have ample resources and you can't rely on an experienced network to guide you through this process. What's more, you may be losing hope and feel disappointed with where you see your life heading—this isn't what you signed up for and it certainly isn't what you envisioned.

Many new or first-generation professionals have been there, and the good news is that there's hope. The principles explored in this book will prove that you *can* have it all without sacrificing who you are or what you care about. As a first generation professional that's been in your shoes and been fortunate enough to learn and benefit from the secrets to success; I'll show you in a clear and candid manner how to obtain the success you want, and provide you with all of the resources you'll need to get it.

NOTHING IN LIFE IS NEW

It's been said that nothing in life is new. For the most part that's true. It's certainly true for the principles I'll share with you. There are other resources that thoroughly describe the concepts contained within this book; in fact some of those resources will be referenced in later chapters or at the end of the book. They provide in-depth analysis or detailed guidance to help you accomplish your personal, professional or financial development goals; however, none of them provide guidance on *all* of these topics in a manner that's uncomplicated, simple to understand and easy to implement.

Even if you don't come across the following principles in another resource, there's nothing that you'll read that someone with a bit of common sense couldn't figure out for themselves. Nevertheless, "common sense" as my Grandma would say, "isn't 'common' to everyone."

Although some are born with the natural ability to succeed, most people achieve success through knowledge that is observed, shared or passed down over a period of time. And while the principles of success can be learned, there's no single path to the truths that I'll share. For example 2 plus 2 equals 4, but so does 3 plus 1, or 7 minus 3. Either way you get there, 4 is still and will always be 4.

That truth is the same for "success"; no matter how you arrive at "success" it's still success. But just because you can "arrive" at success from multiple paths doesn't mean that the journey has to be difficult. What if there's a better or more efficient way of becoming successful? One that doesn't include so many bumps and bruises on the way to achieve it? Over time, I've learned from a host of wildly successful individuals that there is a common theme; a system or set of principles that any person can follow that allows a person to become successful.

Many of these individuals have achieved success before the relatively young age of 35, so their journey seemed shorter than what most would expect. These individuals have started successful and well recognized businesses, or have achieved significant accomplishments in their careers. During the course of our friendship, I've been fortunate to have their secrets to success shared with me.

Their revelations confirmed my theory; many of these individuals had learned or had been passed down similar information about what it takes to become and remain successful. However, what stuck with me and prompted me to share these secrets is that each person felt that they could have achieved success much earlier in their careers if they had been shown, told or taught the secrets to success earlier in their lives!

It's not that these secrets can't be taught; you'll find out shortly that they can. Unfortunately, you're rarely told specifically what you need to do on a personal, professional and financial level to be successful. And if you are told, the instructions are usually focused on a few principles instead of all of the principles, due to the broad scope of issues that must be covered to address all of your personal, professional and financial needs.

THE WISDOM OF OTHERS

The mother of one of my friends had a voicemail introduction that I always thought was cool growing up; and as I got older it became a personal statement of sorts. Her introduction said, "While it's wise to learn from your mistakes, it's wiser to learn from the mistakes of others." Those words had a profound effect on me.

As a teenager and well into my early adult life, I made it my mission to avoid as many mistakes as possible by learning from the mistakes of others. As I developed a better understanding of this wisdom, I began to focus not only on learning from the mistakes of others, but I also used it to learn how successful individuals achieved success.

I'll share those lessons with you in the following pages. The lessons are not new. I don't claim to be the first person to think of them, and at times I may have to refer you to other experts to fill in the specifics of what I haven't experienced personally. Nevertheless, when you're done reading this book, you'll know everything you need to know, just as I've been taught, to be successful personally, professionally and financially.

You may be wondering why you should trust my advice. I'm sure you've thought, "What makes this guy such an expert on success?" Frankly, that's not something I can convince you, especially if we haven't spent enough time together to develop a trusting relationship—one in which you value my advice. All I can do is show the proof in the results after these principles have been applied.

The principles that I'll share have been instrumental in my development from a "C" student at the beginning of high school struggling to gain acceptance to a 4 year college, to an honors undergraduate student, with several exclusive Fortune 500 internships, admitted to a top-20 law school, promoted to a Director-level position in a billion-dollar firm, honored with multiple prestigious professional awards for legal and business leadership, who obtained sought after professorships and national speaking engagements, and a mentor to more than a dozen high-performing emerging leaders—*all by the age of 30.*

I'm confident that if I hadn't been exposed to these principles I'd likely be where the statistics said I'd end up, and where many from my neighborhood ended up—dead, in prison or involved in illegal activities. The good news for you is that none of the results are unique to me. I've seen the principles applied successfully in the lives of countless professionals who've come before and after me. In the following pages I'll reference other successful professionals, from various backgrounds and occupations that are applying these principles in their lives and achieving incredible success personally, professionally and financially. Most importantly, you'll be shown how you can get similar results in a manner that's simple to understand and easy to implement.

DEFINITION OF SUCCESS

Before we go further let's define a critical term in our discussion: success. What is success? Clearly it means different things to different people. As we established earlier, the goal of this book is to learn the principles that allow you to be successful personally, professionally and financially. Keeping that goal in mind, the most appropriate definition of success is the attainment of knowledge, wisdom and health. Not fame, riches and glory.

While it's nice to have all of those things, they are fleeting and can be lost at a moment's notice. Moreover, fame, riches and glory can be difficult if not impossible to regain if they're lost. However, items gained with knowledge, wisdom and health, can be gained, lost and regained again because the key components that led to their acquisition still remain present and can be used to regain the lost item.

DECEPTIVE SIMPLICITY

The principles we'll explore are like most things in life; they are deceptively simple. They are easy to understand, so easy you wonder why everyone's not putting them into action; but they're difficult to do on a regular basis, so most people quit before they achieve substantial results. Don't be alarmed. This is no different than our most common challenge—losing weight.

There are millions of books out there on the subject. The weight loss industry is worth billions of dollars. But at its core, the formula for weight loss is deceptively simple, eat less than you want to, eat and drink more stuff that you don't want to, like veggies and water, and exercise more than you want to. That's simple right? To make it even simpler you could sum it up by telling someone to "take in less calories than you burn off."

So why are there books, tapes and DVD's telling you how to do something so simple? Because, those books, tapes and DVD's are trying to *encourage* you to keep doing the simple thing—some of which you don't want to do, even though it's simple but "feels hard"—so that you can *achieve* the results you want.

GET YOUR MIND RIGHT

Achieving personal, professional and financial success requires the proper mindset. You have to approach these principles with humility and acknowledge that wisdom may be gained from those that have made the journey before you. If you think you have it all figured out, this book is not for you. The principles work because they utilize the wisdom of others. They allow you to learn from others so you can avoid common mistakes that make the path to success more difficult. Does that mean that you can't deviate from what's shared? Sure, you can. However, it's critical that you apply the wisdom of others where appropriate to minimize the challenges you'll face.

Your attitude while applying the principles is just as important as following the principles themselves. You have to believe you've succeeded before you even begin. You need to have the mindset that you can and, more importantly, that you *will* accomplish the goals you'll set for yourself. You must block out the doubt that naturally creeps in, and stop the naysayers dead in their tracks before you even begin the journey. Trust and believe that regardless of what you've done in your past that this will work.

It's guaranteed to work for you if you diligently apply the principles; you just have to have faith in yourself. You owe it to yourself to see this process through to completion—until you achieve success. Don't just perform the tasks suggested in this book; change your outlook. Begin viewing your circumstances differently. Change your outlook so that your mind, or your intellect and your will, controls your destiny; not your emotions or your present circumstances.

You are what you think you are. So instead of focusing on the difficulty of the task at hand ("I've got 4 years left to reach my goals"), start focusing on the simplicity of the task at hand ("I *only* have 4 years left to reach my goals"). Your intellect allows you to implement and do, but your will enables you to push through when everything inside you wants to quit or give up.

Envision accomplishing your goals before it happens. Do this for every activity. Believe in yourself and your ability to accomplish the goals you've set, and remain steadfast until you see your goals accomplished. Don't quit on yourself.

It's not an overnight process. Be diligent and persistent. When you start school, a new job or start a business, your goals seem so far away and so difficult to achieve. However, if you remain diligent and persist you'll achieve the goals you set for yourself. It starts with the proper outlook at the beginning and *during* the journey.

Let's begin.

CHAPTER 2: THE FACTS

What You Don't Know Can Hurt You

Why is it important for you to know the secrets to success? What's the harm if you aren't exposed to them? Some people never learn these principles and they're doing fine, aren't they? There are tons of educated and employed individuals making a great salary; isn't that the definition of success, aren't they living the "American Dream"? The data we'll see below tells another story. It confirms that there's more to success than just getting your education, finding a job and making a decent income. Let's take a closer look.

According to the U.S. Department of Labor, many new and first generation professionals are minorities. Although these individuals experience problems in the labor market that are not measurable; those that are quantified include a tendency to be employed in occupations with high levels of unemployment, due to lower than average education. These factors further limit job opportunities, and typically lead to higher levels of unemployment in these communities. Moreover, the above referenced issues also cause minorities to less likely be employed in management or professional occupations, even though these are the highest paying job categories.

The 2009 U.S. Department of Labor labor force statistics showed that half of the Asian men included in the survey worked in management, professional, and related occupations, compared with 35% of White men, 24% of Black men, and 16% of Hispanic men. In addition, 47% of Asian women surveyed were employed in management, professional and related jobs compared with 41% of White women, 34% of Black women and 25% of Hispanic women. Furthermore the data showed that 59% of Asian men and women had a bachelor's degree or higher, compared with 35% of Whites, 24% of Blacks and 16% of Hispanics.

The employment and educational data further emphasized the earnings disparity between Black or Hispanic workers and Asian or White workers across all major occupational groups. For example, in 2009, median weekly earnings of Asian men was $1,357 and $1,266 for White men working full time in management, professional and related occupations were well above the earnings of Hispanic men at $1,017 and $922 for Black men in the same occupations. Among women the earning gap is generally smaller and in some major occupational categories, earnings levels are fairly close. For example the median weekly earnings for Asian women was $1,097 and $913 for White women working full time in management, professional and related occupations, compared to $800 for Black women and $744 for Hispanic women in the same occupations.

If unaddressed, the problem of high unemployment, limited job opportunities and low pay could grow exponentially given the explosive projected growth of minority communities. The U.S. Census Bureau projects that by 2050 the non-Hispanic single-race white population will be slightly larger at 203.3 million persons than in it was in 2008 when 199.8 million persons were identified. In fact, this group is projected to lose population in the 2030s and 2040s and comprise 46 percent of the total population in 2050, down from 66 percent in 2008.

Meanwhile, the Hispanic population is projected to nearly triple, from 46.7 million to 132.8 million during the 2008 to 2050 period. This segment of the population is projected to double from 15 percent to 30 percent. Thus, nearly one in three U.S. residents will be Hispanic.

The black population is projected to grow as well, increasing from 41.1 million, or 14 percent of the population in

2008, to 65.7 million, or 15 percent in 2050. The Asian population is also projected to climb from 15.5 million to 40.6 million, with its share of the nation's population expected to rise from 5.1 percent to 9.2 percent.

Among the remaining segments of the populations, American Indians and Alaska Natives are projected to rise from 4.9 million to 8.6 million or from 1.6 to 2 percent of the total population. The Native Hawaiian and Other Pacific Islander population is expected to more than double, from 1.1 million to 2.6 million. Finally, the number of people who identify themselves as being of two or more races is projected to more than triple, from 5.2 million to 16.2 million.

Therefore, by 2050 the minority population—everyone except for non-Hispanic, single-race whites—is projected to increase dramatically to 235.7 million out of a total U.S. population of 439 million. However, despite this large population growth many minorities may continue to be under-represented in management and professional occupations, instead of increasing proportionately to their growth in population.

Some have argued that this under-representation is and will continue to be caused by a shortage of available minority professional candidates. However, that "pipeline" argument typically views the symptom and not the problem itself. Those who have studied the issue believe that a lack of qualified candidates is caused by a lack of available role models and the inability to access professional development opportunities. The experts argue that these deficiencies are directly related to the inability of potential candidates to secure well-paying management and professional jobs. This conclusion is supported by a 2005 recruiting industry study which found that most successful minority professionals have special mentoring relationships that gave the professionals insightful prospective not known by the average candidate.

THE WEALTH GAP

The Labor statistics clearly demonstrate that it's not enough to go to college and get a job; you have to move into the ranks of leadership and management. Furthermore, it's not enough to earn a good salary; you need to convert the income made into wealth for your family and for future generations.

Regardless of race, the presence of wealth leads to more wealth, and conversely the lack of wealth perpetuates the same. As we'll discuss in Chapter 6, families that lack wealth have less money to pay for college, less money to invest in business, and have less money to handle unplanned economic challenges since most of their wealth, if it exists, is tied up in a home instead of diversified equities like stocks, bonds and mutual funds. As a result, there is less money to transfer to future generations to begin building wealth.

Consequently, it's critical that you develop leadership and management skills that allow you to generate wealth now and for future generations. To do so, you need to learn the rules. You need to become familiar with the principles that allow you to develop leadership and management skills, and then apply them consistently to everything you do professionally.

What some believed was the principles for success have changed over time. A few decades ago the "social contract" in America provided that if you worked hard and paid your dues, at some point you would achieve success: long-term employment that's satisfying, time and money to spend on and with loved ones, and financial security post-employment through a pension—the American Dream. Now, however, that social contract has had several additional clauses added that require more than just hard work to achieve your dreams as a professional. This new contract requires soft skills, networking, a career plan and a viable personal brand—*in addition to hard work*—to achieve professional success. The status quo has changed. But you can't adapt to this change if you don't know what the new status quo is.

CREATE OR DIE

In an article for the Wall Street Journal, Andy Kessler encouraged professionals to focus on jobs that create significant value to avoid being replaced by cheap labor or automation. The article highlighted what we've all witnessed in travel, telecom and financial services industries in the past several decades; the displacement of once plentiful careers as travel agents, tellers, operators, brokers and traders through technological automation. More importantly two types of workers were identified in lieu of our traditional blue-collar and white-collar distinction: creators and servers.

Mr. Kessler defined creators as the professionals that drove productivity, whereas servers, on the other hand, merely serviced the creators and other servers. Many servers, Mr. Kessler stated, would be replaced by machines, by computers or by cheap labor, but creators would continue to enjoy secure employment since their jobs cannot be performed faster or better by a machine; nor can the value they add be achieved by cheaper human alternatives.

Servers, however, are not found in key management or professional occupations, so they usually are paid less and tend to be the first positions eliminated during a downsizing. Therefore, it's critical that you become a creator. We'll explore further in Chapter 5 how you can be a creator by generating significant value for your organization instead of merely "serving."

CHAPTER 3: TALK TO THE FUTURE YOU

The Power of a Butterfly

Growing up I enjoyed watching science fiction films, especially the films that featured time travel. One of my favorites involved the hero traveling to the future where he'd have to prevent something bad from happening to his future-self. The plot required the hero to socialize with others, but avoid interacting with his future-self at all costs to avoid disturbing the space time continuum. If he did, he'd change the present based on things he learned from the future—only in the movies, right?

As crazy as the premised seemed, it was based on actual scientific theory known as the "butterfly effect." The theory states that a small, seemingly insignificant event in one part of the world can over time have a massive effect in another part of the world. For example, a butterfly flapping its wings in a jungle in South America, may startle a lizard who runs across the jungle floor and scares a monkey who screams loudly and startles a herd of animals who cause a gust of wind to sweep into the ocean and start what becomes a hurricane that eventually makes it's way to the East-coast of the United States causing over $5 Billion dollars in property damage. The theory suggests that the massive damage can be attributed to the lone butterfly flapping its wings days earlier.

In scientific circles the "butterfly effect" is a theory, or an unproven idea. Even though many believe it *could* happen, it's difficult to be certain that the seemingly insignificant act is the cause. Those who are successful, however, vigorously disagree with scientists who believe that the "butterfly effect" is merely a theory. Successful professionals know that the "butterfly effect" exists, because they've talked to who they will become in the future!

Ok, wait. Don't stop reading. I'm not crazy. This will all make sense in a minute.

What if you could talk to yourself in the future? What would you ask, what would you want to know? Successful professionals have these conversations frequently during the course of their careers. And they focus most, if not, all of their questions on what they need to do in the present to become successful in the future. They also ask for guidance so that they can avoid or navigate challenges that may prevent their future success.

How do they do this? Do they have some type of black hole that everyone else doesn't know about, or some type of time machine that makes this whole process easier? No. They find a mentor. Someone who they aspire to be like...wait for it...in the future—their *future-self.*

They may meet once, periodically, or frequently with their mentor; but during their time together, the person seeking success attempts to get as much information as he or she can about what the mentor did to become successful. Time is also spent asking the mentor what things the mentor wishes he or she could do differently to avoid problems on their path to success.

SETTING YOUR VISION

A mentor is extremely important in your pursuit of success. They are not just some old person that you're supposed to find and discuss how to get a job, or how to get into a college or a graduate program. When properly selected, you have the unique chance to ask your future-self, someone who you would like to be in the future, what you should be doing now to get to where they are. A mentor can help you set your vision for the future. They can provide you with guidance on how long you can expect to accomplish a specific goal, what to do to avoid challenges in your path, and shed light on what will life be like once you achieve your goal to help manage your expectations. A mentor has the answers to all of these questions because they've already experienced these things; they're currently living the life you want to live!

The role of a mentor in setting your vision is critical to your success. A vision isn't just a dream or hopeful aspiration to successful people. Successful individuals think of visions as plans. They use visions to establish goals then work towards accomplishing those goals.

Mentoring is extremely important to your success because it reduces the risk or uncertainty involved in making a decision that impacts your professional goals. Nothing makes a goal seem less daunting and more plausible than knowing that it can and _has_ been done. As any financial expert will tell you, decreasing your risk conversely improves the return or reward on the investment you're making—that's why you usually weigh the risks and rewards before making a decision. The advice of a mentor increases the positive outcome of the decision you're making by using your mentor to advise you on how to avoid failure or potential challenges in your path.

If you don't believe me, let's consider that you've already graduated from high school and while there, you played on a state championship football team as the star quarterback. If you're approached shortly after graduation by an eighth grader who's curious about what it takes to play on the same high school football team and win the State Championship; wouldn't you say that you could easily tell the kid what to do and what not to do if he wants to follow in your footsteps? Sure, you could. You could easily tell the kid what your training schedule was, how you prepared for games, how the games felt while you were playing them, and ultimately what it feels like to be a state champion and all the benefits you've received since winning the "big game."

What your mentor shares with you is no different than what you'd share in the example above. Only, instead of talking about football, your mentor would give a detailed overview and description of the specific professional experience that he or she has had: what is was like getting promoted from Manager, to Director, to Executive Vice President, what he or she did to gain such promotions, what he or she read, what advanced training he or she received or what social or industry groups he or she participated in.

By the end of your discussion with your mentor, assuming you still aspire to follow the same path as this individual, your vision should be formed. You should have clearly identified goals to pursue—books or magazines to read, classes to take or training to obtain, and groups to join. Once you have your path clearly identified by your mentor you will know who the key companies, organizations, experts, educational resources, websites, etc. are in that field, and you'll have clear insight on how to pursue or join them. All of the steps will be described for you, no guesswork involved, ready to be followed; further proving the point that you don't have to be smart, you just have to know who to copy!

Although the process is simple, you'll still have to take personal responsibility for your goals and career development instead of relying on your mentor or someone else like your academic counselor or your boss. But at least you'll have a starting point and a path to guide the way. The path described by your mentor will be your benchmark. It will let you know where you can or should be as you progress in your development. It will also help you to navigate unfamiliar territory with confidence and allow you to get comfortable with being in uncomfortable or unknown situations.

MEETING MY FUTURE-SELF

My vision of success was formed, shaped and modified over time, but the approach has always remained the same. I found my future-self and asked as many questions as I could to find out how my mentor achieved the success I sought. The process began towards the end of high school when I participated in a science internship at a large multinational consumer products company in the Twin Cities. During my internship I made sure that I spent at least 30 minutes a week with my boss, a Manager in the department, and asked him as many questions as I could about how he got his current position. I didn't want his job, but I wanted his lifestyle. I wanted to be able to get paid for my intellectual talents rather than my manual labor. I wanted to be a creator rather than a server.

I would formally schedule time to meet or informally ask him out to lunch or to grab a cup of coffee, and use the opportunity to ask questions about what I had observed since our last meeting. I would pepper him with questions regarding his "typical" work day; what formal or informal training he had received to prepare him for his role, what obstacles he faced while moving from a new hire to experienced employee and what he recalled doing to overcome obstacles during his journey.

Over time, as our relationship developed, he began volunteering information about his path to success without me asking. He also began taking me along to meetings he thought would benefit my professional development or forwarding me books and articles to read to improve whatever skill we had discussed during our previous meeting. By the end of the internship we had developed an excellent rapport and he was now fully vested in my professional development.

While back at school, I would check in with him from time to time to give him progress reports and to keep him informed of my professional growth and development. Without fail, the more I kept in touch and keep him apprised of what I was up to, the more he continued to invest in me.

I came to find that the process didn't change much with each mentor relationship I developed over the next fifteen years. I would find a mentor, build our relationship through frequent interaction where I would ask and probe further into how my mentor became successful, and I'd provide periodic feedback to my mentor about how I applied their advice to a given situation and inform them of the results obtained from doing so. Through this process, each mentor would increase their level of involvement in my professional development and help to guide me on my path to success.

FINDING A MENTOR

In light of the importance of having a mentor, you may be wondering, "how do I find a mentor?" It's actually quite simple, all you have to do is identify someone you admire for a given set of skills or qualities and ask them to spend time with you in a formal or informal setting that you both share in common. That's it.

You don't have to ask them to be your mentor; you don't have to indicate that you're looking for a mentor-mentee relationship. It can be as simple as asking this person to grab coffee with you, or meet for breakfast or lunch—everyone eats and drinks so you can't get more "in-common" than that. You're also not limited to these options, feel free to mix it up and do something more your style if you know they may be interested as well. For example, if both of you are into sports, invite them to a game if you have an extra ticket. If you're into outdoor activities and they are too, ask them to join you next time you hunt, fish, bike, or run; just make the offer to spend time participating in a common interest—all they can say is "no."

Once you've identified the person you'd like to be your mentor and you've asked them to participate in an activity you both have in common, then give some thought to what you would like to get out of your meeting. Because you want to make this the first of many encounters, you should try to give the prospective mentor an idea of who you are, what your interests are and why you wanted to meet him or her. Let the prospective mentor know what you admire about them and what you'd like to learn from them. Needless to say, all of this should be communicated in an informal manner, you don't want to seem pushy or needy. The last thing you want to do is to scare the person away before they get to know you.

Your first few meetings should avoid significant requests. Spend time asking questions about the individual and demonstrate an interest in how and what they have done professionally; don't ask for items that, excluding advice, benefits you. Most mentors will be happy to share their life experience and tell you all that they know if they believe that you will actually implement the advice they are giving you, and if they believe that you don't have ulterior motives beyond the advice they are giving.

Why would a person mentor you? What's in it for them? Why wouldn't they keep the information you're seeking to themselves; after all, you could become a threat in the future or use the information to gain a competitive advantage over her. To answer these questions let's examine your role as a mentee; what are you doing, or more importantly, what are you asking the mentor to do?

A mentee encourages the mentor to do what most of us love doing—talk about oneself. Think about it, does someone have to "twist your arm" to make you talk about yourself. No, you can easily spend hours talking about who you are, why you're so awesome and how you got that way. Talking about yourself doesn't require much, if any, begging and pleading to get the subject to cooperate. This is why most mentors are happy to meet with you again and again—to talk about themselves. It's a gentle ego-stroke. You, as the mentee, willingly "sit at the feet of the master" and ask away, and in exchange, the master of what you need to know spends time enthusiastically telling you what they know.

Of course a mentor's reasons for sharing their expertise with you isn't limited to hearing themselves talk. While they may like to talk about themselves and how they got to where they are; many mentors are just as motivated, if not more, by the desire to have you participate in the spoils of success. Successful people generally want to see others successful. Why? Because it's no fun being at a party all-alone—the more the merrier! Some mentors even have the ultimate altruistic motives—they understand and have experienced first-hand the power of these success principles and as a way of "giving back", they want to have the personal satisfaction of seeing the principles work for you. Think about it, that's the purpose of this book.

Those who know and apply the secrets to success understand their effectiveness. We could have kept the principles a closely guarded secret, but that's not how it works. The principles were shared with us, so we must share them with others. That's why most mentors do what they do—someone took the time to mentor them. Hopefully, as you develop, you'll take time to give back as well and share what you've learned. You'll "go back in time" for someone and speak to your past, as the future-self for someone else, and set in motion a chain of events that no one could foresee; you'll be a butterfly effect in someone's life.

BENEFITS OF MENTORING

Mentoring provides benefits beyond "feel-good" moments. Researchers have proven that mentoring can significantly aid in leadership and management development and increase your earning potential. Both educational and occupational studies have indicated that students and employees are more likely to succeed if they have a mentor. A key finding is that professionals who experienced limited growth in management lacked a connection to their mentor and received mentoring that was purely instructional and focused primarily on skill development. However, professionals who excelled in management and rose to executive levels enjoyed closer and fuller developmental relationships with their mentors, especially early in the executive's career when the individual needed to build confidence, credibility, and competence.

According to Triple Creek, a leader in enterprise mentoring technology, more than 75% of executives have stated that mentoring played a critical role in their successful careers. Such statements have been validated by additional surveys, which confirm that professionals who have had strong mentoring relationships can annually earn between $5,000 and $22,000 more than those who have not had successful mentoring relationships. Forget the warm and fuzzy feelings, successful mentoring can produce cold hard cash.

Studies have also found that mentor's who help their mentee's build large networks of experienced advisors that are diverse in professional occupations, positions, experience, location, function and demographics, better prepare the mentee for leadership and executive management roles by introducing the mentee to guidance from a variety of wise individuals. Each of these individuals serves as an additional point of contact to help the mentee get to the next level in their career.

To have a beneficial mentoring relationship your mentor has to create an environment similar to a structured apprenticeship. You need to observe and participate in the task or skill being taught, and see how your mentor accomplishes the task or demonstrates the skill. Then you can attempt to perform the same task or master the skill taught, and benchmark your results against your mentor.

One of my earliest professional mentors was a well-known lawyer who ended up serving on the Minnesota Supreme Court. Under his tutelage I learned how to write effectively and persuasively by literally sitting by his side and watching him in action. He would provide me with articles to review and revise, and after doing so, he would sit next to me at a table and show me how he would have revised the same article. In the process, he would not only make revisions but more importantly, he would explain why he was making the changes he made. He would take time to explain what he wanted to convey to the reader with the revisions made, so I could get inside his mind and fully understand what he was doing.

In contrast, some of the worst mentoring experiences I've had involved situations where a "mentor" would merely provide general feedback with little or no explanation as to why the individual did what they did. Worse yet, the ineffective mentor would use generic terms like "think outside the box" or "stretch yourself" to attempt to clarify the corrective measures I needed to take to improve my work product. Such feedback is not bad in and of itself; however, the mentor failed to realize that those clichés mean very little to someone who hasn't achieved the results that "outside the box" or "stretched" thinking creates.

The ineffective mentor never stopped to consider, "what does this mean to someone who hasn't done it before?"

Nor did he consider, "how should the mentee do this?" or "How would I do it?" An effective mentor instructs or guides from the mentee's perspective. If yours doesn't, gently remind them that you haven't performed the activity before and that it would be helpful if they could teach you from that perspective. Ensure that you have an opportunity to participate or observe your mentor in action, if appropriate. And when you are allowed to observe, ask your mentor to explain *what* you're supposed to be learning or observing to ensure that you're getting the most from the experience.

For example, does your mentor want you to see how to prepare for or lead a meeting? Are you being allowed to participate to hear what terms or phrases are used when presenting to leaders within your organization? Knowing what you're supposed to learn from the experience allows you to "play with the house's money" by observing or participating in an inactive role or simulated environment where there's nothing at stake, or little to no pressure on you.

Even though you're an inactive participant you should prepare or participate as though you are your mentor for the given activity. Think of what you would say or do and then compare it to what actually happened. Doing so will help you to develop superior skills in a safe and supportive environment, and better prepares you for the challenges you'll face when you're presented with the same situation.

Although mentoring clearly benefits the mentor and the mentee, a third beneficiary is the mentee's company. According to Triple Creek, companies receive many positive benefits when its employees are effectively mentored; including increased recruitment, retention and employee productivity. In fact, more than 60% of college and graduate students listed mentoring as criteria for selecting an employer after graduation.

With respect to retention, 77% of companies reported that mentoring programs were effective in increasing retention. Companies with successful mentoring programs had 20% lower employee turnover than those that didn't offer such programs, and 35% of employees who did not receive regular mentoring began looking for another job within 12 months of joining their current company. Finally, the study showed that managerial productivity increased by 88% when mentoring was present versus 24% with training alone, and 95% of survey respondents said that they were motivated to do their best when working because of the mentoring received.

It's clear from the abundance of research on this issue that successful professionals utilize mentors to effectively develop and execute their career goals. Moreover, the findings clearly demonstrate that effective mentoring allows you to develop sought-after leadership and management skills, leading to increased earning potential and high-levels of job security.

Therefore, find a good mentor, set your vision and continue to lean on their wisdom and understanding to achieve your goals of personal, professional and financial success.

CHAPTER 4: EDUCATION PRINCIPLES

Start early, learn often, and get the most bang for your buck

If success is attained through knowledge, wisdom and health, it's clear that education plays a key role in at least one, if not two of the three primary contributors to success. Education is important because it allows you to obtain knowledge; however, true education isn't limited solely to what you obtain, it's based upon what you *retain*.

You don't have to seek knowledge in a formal institution to obtain or retain it. You can acquire knowledge anywhere including books, blogs, seminars, or from working or volunteering. And while some institutions such as four-year colleges or universities provide a great way to facilitate this process, there are various alternatives to the typical educational institutions such as professional, vocational or trade schools that provide excellent educational opportunities.

Nevertheless most professional careers require some form of formal education, whether it be through a post-secondary program, community college, undergraduate college or university, or post-graduate program. Regardless of which route you take to acquire a formal education the objective is the same; finish as quick as you can, for the least amount of money, while attending the best program you can afford and be admitted to. Doing so provides the best value for your educational dollar.

Sadly, many students aren't getting the most for their educational dollar. A recent survey showed that approximately 47% of the entering students at the average four-year college takes more than six years to graduate. Even more troubling is that respondents to the American Enterprise Institute survey of over 1,400 schools had a significant number of schools with rates between 60% and 70%.

There are numerous reasons that cause a student to take more than 4 years to graduate, including a lack of adequate funds, a family crisis, transferring schools, switching majors or choosing a double major. However, the cost of delaying graduation can be substantial given the amount of income lost by not working after four years, plus the higher cost of tuition and fees for each additional year of schooling.

And while it's important to obtain a great education, it's more important that you can afford your education once you graduate; otherwise, you may find yourself no better off financially than if you hadn't pursued your degree. Fully assess the cost of your education and take necessary measures to ensure that your costs remain low. Failure to do so may burden you with large student loans that make pursuing your dreams difficult because you'll be too focused on debt repayment.

A survey conducted by the Project on Student Debt relying on data from the U.S. Department of Education found that 62% of graduates of public universities had student loans averaging $20,200. The figures at private non-profit universities were 72% and $27,650 respectively. Interestingly, the average student-debt increased by 20% at public universities, from $16,850 in 2004, and student-debt grew by 29% at private non-profit universities where the average was $21,500. More distressing was the fact that Pell Grant recipients, or those who generally have family incomes under $50,000, had an average debt of $24,800 or nearly $2,000 more than the average for all seniors graduating with loans.

Unlike undergraduate tuition costs, graduate school tuition can vary greatly depending on the type of graduate program a student chooses, so it's difficult to accurately compare student-loan debt. While MBA programs tend to be the most expensive, it's not uncommon with top-tier programs raising tuition faster than inflation for graduate programs, for public or private institutions to range from $10,000 to $40,000 per year, along with the additional $10,000 - $20,000 for room and board, books and transportation.

Although such costs can be high, many graduate programs offer stipends that cover tuition, living expenses and even a small salary for students earning a master's or PhD in exchange for student research or teaching. Furthermore, many graduate students may qualify for tuition reimbursement from their employer. Regardless of these variances in cost the value principle for graduate programs remains the same as undergraduate programs: finish as quick as you can, for the least amount of money, while attending the best program you can afford and be admitted to.

There are many online calculators that can help you determine whether you can afford to pay for your undergraduate or graduate program after graduation. These calculators can easily tell you how long it will take you to repay your student loans, as well as estimate the monthly costs of repayment. Though the initial cost of repayment may seem low, don't forget to factor in your cost of living expenses such as housing, food, and transportation; if you don't know how to do so, Chapter 6 provides an excellent budgetary overview.

In addition to seeking value, it's critical to choose an institution that allows you to gain entry into your chosen profession, and through an average salary, allows you to repay any student loans you may have obtained while going to school. Don't be fooled by high salary figures shown in recruiting materials. Focus on what the average graduate from your school who majors in the same courses makes after graduation.

Every school will post these figures in some fashion. However, confirm that the data you're provided is supported by figures from recent graduates. What they're making is likely what you'll make since it's more current than the information provided in recruiting materials that may be outdated. Also, review online job sites and classified ads to confirm starting salaries in your profession. This will help you honestly assess whether you'll be able to repay your student loans after graduation.

A review of the National Association of Colleges and Employers 2011 Spring Salary Survey confirms that the average salary for all graduates in 2011 is more than $50,000. Business majors received an average salary of $48,089, with engineering graduates and technology disciplines receiving $59,435 and $61,783, respectively. Liberal Arts majors received the lowest salaries on average as a group at $35,633.

Based on the current data, failing to get the most value out of your education can be a costly mistake. Using the average salary figures, the failure to graduate within 4 years could cost you a minimum of $80,000 per year for each year you delay graduation; including room and board, increased tuition, transportation and lost earnings.

HOW TO MAXIMIZE EDUCATIONAL VALUE

Given the potentially massive losses that can occur if you don't maximize the value of your education, you have to start the process of selecting a school early and research each component of the educational equation to ensure your success.

How many times have you heard of someone going to school for two or three years longer than their program requires, only to graduate and still not be able to find work in their chosen field? Usually, that means that they've incurred more debt than planned to complete their studies and now they can't generate enough income through the entry-level job taken post-graduation to meet their financial needs. This typically leads to the individual questioning whether they made the right decision to pursue their current career.

The result can be avoided with proper planning early in the decision making process. First, you need to determine what you want to do before you begin the program. That seems intuitive, but you'd be surprised how many people begin their post-secondary studies without having a basic idea of what they want to do after graduation. This isn't limited to undergraduate studies, many post-graduate students fall victim to the same lack of planning. They go through all of the hurdles of getting admitted into a program without fully deciding what they want to do with the degree once they're done. While you don't need to know exactly what you want to do, or have your choices limited to a single plan; you should at least have a clear and practical idea of what opportunities await you once you've completed your studies based on data from recent graduates.

Once you have an idea of what you want to do when you've finished your program, the next thing to do is to research the best institutions for that field. Check out U.S. News and World Report's undergraduate and graduate program rankings or Barron's Profiles of American Colleges. Visit the program's website, call and speak to admissions counselors, visit their facilities and speak to recent graduates if you can. Try to confirm if your expectations match the reality of currently enrolled students. For example, if you expect to make $50,000 when you graduate but none of the recent graduates you've talked to are making anything close to that, you may want to re-evaluate your decision or pick a different institution to research.

After you've completed your research and confirmed that the institution can help you gain employment in your chosen profession, minimize your student loan borrowing by employing some or all of the following cost reduction strategies suggested by the U.S. Department of Education:

- Apply for merit or non-need based scholarships if you received good grades prior to enrollment.

- Research whether your school offers special discounts, grants or scholarships for children of alumni; for multiple enrolled siblings; or for particular talents or enrollment in particular programs (e.g., music, drama, journalism, etc.).

- Ask about reciprocity or tuition matching if your school is similar to another program nearby. This is typically granted to students attending from a neighboring state or by private schools seeking to attract students considering the nearby public college or university.

- Investigate if financial assistance is offered if one of your parents, especially the major wage earner, is unemployed. In addition, many schools set aside financial aid for those who fail to qualify for state or federal aid.

- Attend a community college for a year or two to take advantage of lower tuition costs, and then transfer to a 4-year institution.

- Save as much as $6,000 per year by living at home to reduce room and board costs; or investigate free or reduced housing options through your municipality's public housing program or your school's resident advisor program.

- Consider participating in a Reserve Officers Training Corps (ROTC) scholarship program. These programs cover tuition and textbook costs and provide a monthly living stipend in exchange for a service commitment after graduation.

- Find out if your parent's employer offers tuition assistance for the child of an employee. Many times you may find that grants or scholarships are offered that go unused because no one takes advantage of this little known opportunity.

Once enrolled, focus on getting the best grades you can. Again, this is self-explanatory, but must be said. Many individuals get into great programs, but end up doing so poorly employers overlook them when they apply for jobs. Avoid this from occurring by constantly assessing where you are in your courses. Ask for help if you begin falling behind or not getting the grades you want on assignments and tests. The earlier you ask for and receive help, the better your chances are of getting good grades in the class.

Find free resources at your school that will help you with the courses you find challenging, but don't forget the best resource of all—your instructor. No one knows the materials better than the person teaching it. Call, email or visit during office hours and ask for the instructor's help. Be as specific as possible with your questions to ensure that you're given the right answers and shown the correct method to solve the problem on your own.

Outside of the classroom, try to gain as much practical experience as you can in your area of focus. Determine the skills and qualifications for the jobs you want, and then seek to gain relevant experience and establish mentoring relationships.

Volunteer, join social clubs, intern or gain part-time or seasonal employment before graduation with an employer in your field. The more experience you can gain, the better prepared you'll be after graduation. Don't limit your search for experience to external employers. You can gain valuable experience on campus as well. Find departments that employ professionals with your skill and try to obtain a student job where you can learn and observe the professional environment you want to work in after graduation.

Also, serve on student boards, groups or organizations that allow you to further develop the skills you'll need post-graduation. Many of these student led groups are wonderful opportunities for you to demonstrate leadership in your chosen profession while gaining the necessary skills for your post-graduate career.

Whether at work, through an internship, or through a volunteer or student organization, you will have various opportunities to meet and network with individuals in your desired profession. Utilize the opportunity to demonstrate the skills you've obtained when interacting with these individuals. Think of each interaction as an informal interview to showcase your knowledge and talent. It may lead to a job after graduation; but even if it doesn't, it allows you an opportunity to build solid referral networks with individuals you can call on for leads or references when you need them.

If the current organization doesn't have the individuals you want to meet, look up the persons you want to meet online. Review their professional biography on LinkedIn or through a Google search to see what skills and experiences they've acquired. Once you know, you can develop a plan to acquire those skills as well.

Remember to take advantage of the services offered by your career services office. Utilize their job boards or job banks to help you find employment in your chosen profession. Get assistance preparing your resume and cover letter for jobs you're interested in. Leverage any insights or personal connections to alumni they may have for companies where you are applying. Ask for interview tips or request a practice interview to help you prepare and make the best first impression you can. You have paid for this service as part of your tuition, so make the most of it.

CHOOSING A CAREER

Maximizing value may seem easy once you know the principles to apply. However, many people struggle with picking a career that's right for them; after all, it's such a daunting task. It's what you'll do day in and day out for the rest of your life! Don't be frightened by the magnitude of the decision. Picking your career is as simple as the old saying goes: "do what you love and the money will follow."

It's extremely simplistic, but it's true. You may not agree if you've tried doing what you "love" and never experienced money chasing after you. However, in those situations what I've observed is that many people confused "love" with "like" when it came to their professional aspirations. As Simon Sinek commented in his influential TED presentation, "How Great Leaders Inspire Action," people who chose a career based on what they like, or because they can do the job, will work for a paycheck; but people who choose a career because they love performing the related service or making the associated product will pour everything they have into their job.

Passionate professionals generate more income, or have money "follow" them, than those that aren't because they rise to the top of their profession. As we'll see in Chapter 5 these individuals are passionate about adding value to their organization, and their passion propels them to the high-paying management and leadership ranks. Although you can make it to the top without passion, it's hard to *remain* there for a long period if you're not passionate about what you're doing, given the demands on you and your time.

When you're passionate about something you put in extra time and go above and beyond what's required of you because you truly enjoy what you're doing. You're attitude is positive and you look for ways to improve your performance because you genuinely enjoy the tasks assigned; you find the task pleasurable. This is what allows the money to "follow" you. It leads to great work that in turn allows for greater promotional opportunities and ultimately leads to increased income.

Therefore, make sure when you're choosing a profession to focus on what you love instead of merely what you *like*. Identify areas of interest that you find easy—not that there aren't any challenges—but focus on things you can do effortlessly even when challenges arise. This is the most basic indication of where your talents lie.

Bo Burlingham, former Editor at Large of Inc. Magazine wrote in his book *Small Giants: Companies that Choose to be Great Instead of Big*, that a business person is an artist, one that uses both sides of his brain; and that his expression is his business. He said that a businessperson looks at a problem and sees what everyone else is missing. His definition isn't limited to just entrepreneurs; all professionals—those that love what they do—have this gift.

They can see an engineering, accounting, medical, legal, or human resources problem and find the solution that the average employee, whether or not they hold the same title, is missing. These professionals express their solution in an awe-inspiring building, financial statement, medical diagnosis, or agreement.

You've heard professional athletes express a similar concept after an amazing performance. When interviewed, the athlete will state that the game just slowed down and he was allowed to see and react to things differently than his other competitors. This is known as the "zone." An athlete in the zone will see what everyone else can't and seem to know what to do and how to do it before anyone else can react. This leads to magical performances where legends are made and records are broken.

Make your own legend and break records in your respective field by avoiding the pursuit of money, and instead pursue your passion; the money will follow.

CHAPTER 5: PROFESSIONAL PRINCIPLES

Professional Success is Easy as P.I.E.

You've made it. You've networked, acquired knowledge and gained experience to get to this level. You're a professional. However, as we explored in Chapter 2, none of this is a guarantee for success. Most of your colleagues are smart, talented and hard working, that's why they're here. To distinguish yourself and advance within your organization you need to develop management and leadership skills that drive productivity and create value for your clients or customers, your superiors, and your organization. Failure to do so may lead to a "dead-end" job or could lead to your role being eliminated. To avoid these pitfalls you need to focus on what you know, what you show, and where that information flows—don't worry, it's as easy as P.I.E.

EASY AS P.I.E.

The path to professional success starts by recognizing that you're a brand, whether you like it or not. Your brand consists of your image, or what people see and expect or what you tell them to expect. It also consists of the experience people have when they interact with you, including what they receive or what you deliver during those interactions. To be successful, ensure that your brand image and brand experience consistently aligns in a positive way for clients or customers, supervisors and others stakeholders associated with your organization.

I've seen many people try to quantify the relationship between your brand image and your brand experience, but none have done it quite as masterfully as a presentation I attended recently where the presenters referenced the "P.I.E." theory.

P.I.E. is an acronym for Performance, Image and Exposure. This theory asserts that your career success depends upon your ability to perform excellently and convey the proper image, while being seen by those who have influence over your career. It states that 10% of your success is attributed to performance, 30% to your image, and the remaining 60% of your success can be attributed to your exposure. The theory, while controversial to some, has been widely taught by consulting firms, major corporations and featured prominently in *Empowering Yourself: The Organizational Game Revealed* by an author of no relation, Harvey J. Coleman.

While some may debate the degree to which performance, image and exposure impact an individual's career success; it's difficult to deny that they are key contributors to your success. Regardless of the ratios, it's clear that you have to do great work on each project and focus on high-value tasks rather than routine and mundane activities to achieve professional success. In addition, you have to deliver results that exceed expectations, and assist your company with internal and external thought leadership.

The image you convey has to align with the experience you provide when someone interacts with you. You have to look and act the part to get the part. It is easier to get promoted if your superiors envision you in the role. For example, receiving a managerial promotion requires you not only to produce like a manager, but you have to dress and act like a manager also. Thus, pay attention to what your managers are reading, observe how they dress, and take note of how they communicate. Assuming you're performing at a high level, adopting these traits will help you to convey to your superiors that you're fully prepared to advance to the next level.

Remember, your brand image includes not only how you look, but also how you communicate. It is not solely limited to what people expect, but what you tell them to expect; it includes clear communication. You can possess the most intelligent ideas, but if you can't convey them to others within your organization, your ideas won't have a chance to become a reality. Lee Iacocca, the former President and CEO of Chrysler, remarked that ideas often fail to get approved at companies, not due to the quality of the idea, but because of the quality of the communication. All great ideas will fail if not properly communicated, so learn to take complex issues, ideas and strategies, and make them simple and easy to understand by your audience.

Finally, ensure that all of your hard work is seen by key stakeholders within and outside of your organization; including supervisors, influential managers, mentors, and other professionals in your network. You can't be promoted to the next level if no one knows what you're doing or what you've done.

A major misinterpretation of the P.I.E. theory asserts that performance is not important and places greater emphasis on gaining exposure, instead of doing great work. Not only is that understanding flawed, it will likely lead to disastrous results—like getting fired. When used correctly the P.I.E. theory encourages you to do a great job on every project. Such stellar performance allows you to get promoted to the next position.

It all starts with performing great work. If you're not doing good work or providing a good brand experience, your brand image and your brand experience will not align. And ultimately, you'll have nothing to gain exposure or recognition for. Worse yet, if you do gain exposure, it will be because of your failure to align expectations with what you ultimately produced.

We've briefly introduced principles that impact your professional success. Let's further explore the various methods you can use to improve your performance, enhance your image and gain significant exposure to influential people within and outside of your organization, to achieve professional success.

SUCCESS IS A SKILL THAT CAN BE LEARNED

Professional success starts with doing great work that demonstrates your expertise in something that has real or tangible value. Don't worry if you're not an expert now, the good news is that you can learn to become one over time.

Anders Ericsson, a professor who focuses on expert performance, has written extensively on the subject of learned greatness. As co-author of the nine hundred and eighteen page treatise, *The Cambridge Handbook of Expertise and Expert Performance,* he concluded that elite performers are not genetically superior, as some typically believe. Instead he found that they deliberately "practice success" until they become successful at the skill or trait that they are trying to master. He further demonstrated that, with the exception of a few athletic events, no characteristic of the brain or body limits an individual from reaching an expert level.

According to Professor Ericsson, successful people do things differently from those who find success elusive. Successful people have different practice histories. They engage in what he calls "deliberate practice"—an effortful activity designed to improve performance.

In observing deliberate practice, Professor Ericsson noticed that successful people practiced above and beyond the minimum required time, vigorously analyzed what they did right and wrong, focused on ways to eliminate their mistakes, then practiced in a deliberate manner to eliminate those mistakes. The testing and analysis phases were continuously repeated, and progress was documented by individuals to better understand how and when they improved.

Professor Ericsson's research draws striking parallels to the Japanese business process improvement known as Kaizen. The process, which can be translated as good change or improvement, seeks to incrementally improve a process over time through constant evaluation of the outcome versus the desired goal. A core principle of Kaizen is feedback, or the self-reflection process; and its critical purpose is to identify, reduce and ultimately eliminate unwanted outcomes from a given process. The focus is always on incremental gains rather than large changes. Over time, however, such incremental gains lead to radical changes that achieve desired outcomes while minimizing unwanted results.

In addition to the support provided by the Kaizen process, Professor Ericsson's research has been further popularized by Malcolm Gladwell in his best-selling book *Outliers: The Story of Success*. In the book, Mr. Gladwell summarizes Ericsson's research by establishing the ten thousand hour rule; that is, greatness may be achieved in any activity if you spend more than ten thousand hours practicing the activity. Whether the rule is a hard and fast number is for academics to debate. What's relevant is that success can be obtained if you deliberately practice it over a period of years. You have to push yourself beyond where you think your limit is, Mr. Gladwell suggests; each time paying close attention to how and why you've failed, and then seek to correct those failures through more practice.

Ericsson, Gladwell and the Kaizen process prove that you can obtain success through deliberate practice and incremental improvement. You have to develop hypotheses about your limitations, conduct experiments and track the data to analyze what you're doing incorrectly, and then work to improve your failures. Treat each failure as an opportunity to learn and improve, and ultimately, view the failure as a step closer to realizing your success. As England's historic Prime Minister Winston Churchill said, "A pessimist sees the difficulty in every opportunity, but an optimist sees the opportunity in every difficulty."

THE ART OF SELF-ASSESSMENT

Professional success is obtained through candid self-assessment. You have to know what you're weaknesses are. If you're surprised by other's critiques or criticisms, then you probably aren't being candid enough. Assess your skills or performance critically from the perspective of a neutral party. Consider what you liked or disliked about your performance and assess how you can improve. Always evaluate your skills or performances based on the highest standard available and seek to meet that standard.

Constantly evaluate your skills and performance, focusing more on what you've done wrong and once identified, systematically work to correct those failures. When you've achieved a level of expertise, move to your next weakest area and address that weakness. Over time, you should

have fewer areas of weakness and many more areas of
expertise. This increases your likelihood of doing great
work on each project you've been assigned, and allows
you to gain exposure internally and externally as an expert
in those areas.

Most people focus on what they are strongest in and
ignore their weaknesses. Successful persons reverse this
process to be well rounded in all areas. Spend a significant
amount of time practicing what you're not good at, so you
can improve your weaknesses and develop strength over
time in multiple areas. Remember, you're a *professional*—
someone who's mastered many areas of their chosen
occupation.

Start practicing your skills in small, informal or familiar
settings like community and volunteer activities, or
smaller less visible projects at work. Take notes of your
performance, assess, debrief, and set specific goals for
improvement following the next opportunity. Keep
repeating the process until you achieve the desired result
and minimize unwanted outcomes, and you've mastered
the skill or activity.

My self-assessment process includes studying the profiles
of successful individuals. I love reading "top" lists or
"who's who" lists to gain inspiration from what others
have accomplished, or by learning about what they're

doing. I've used such lists to develop best practices, to chart my career path, and to benchmark my performance against those I admire. This process allows me to never become "great" in my own mind. It always shows me something I can improve. Seeing the accomplishments of these individuals is a humbling reminder of all that I have left to achieve, and helps me to focus on future possibilities instead of past achievements.

I also seek incremental improvement by attempting to surround myself with successful individuals from various industries, dissimilar ages and differing ethnicities. The constant presence of these individuals in my life helps me to stay focused on my professional goals by surrounding me with driven and ambitious individuals, and helps to push me to excel each time I hear about the fantastic progress made by one of these individuals.

Studies suggest that your personal success may be a reflection of the average of the five persons with whom you spend the most time. Whether or not such conclusions can be empirically proven, it's clear that you are the company you keep. If you have close acquaintances in your life that are striving to achieve success, it's only natural that you will likely follow the same path as well. Conversely, if you are the most accomplished person in your personal network, it's probable that you may not strive to do more since you've already "made it" in your mind—it causes you to remain stagnant.

Long before the research of Anders Ericsson or Malcolm
Gladwell, arguably one of man-kind's pound-for-pound
greatest physical specimens, Bruce Lee, understood that
to be successful you couldn't stay stagnant. Mr. Lee
famously said, "There are no limits. There are plateaus,
and you must not stay there; you must go beyond them. If
it kills you, it kills you." Keep pushing yourself towards
greatness, it won't kill you.

WHAT ARE YOU OFFERING?

A critical part of your self-assessment is knowing what
you have to offer to others. If you're a brand, what's your
brand statement; who are you and what do you offer?
Answering this question will help you to understand the
product you're marketing—you; and further allow you to
gain exposure by clearly telling others about what you can
do for them.

For example, if you are an accountant you may view your
product as "accounting" or related to the practice of
accounting. That's not incorrect, but it's likely incomplete.
The skills you offer make up the practice of accounting
but it's likely comprised of much more—not only do you
review and analyze financial documents, but you likely
advise and counsel clients on how to implement certain
recommendations to improve their financial situation.

Given the skills you bear your product could be described as "providing experienced financial reporting, analysis and cash management services."

Coming up with a fancy description is not the goal. Regardless of what your brand statement is, if you offer it you have to deliver, or your marketing is in vain and you have lost all credibility with that person. Worse yet, that person will tell others and ultimately people won't believe your brand statement.

The skills you offer should solve a need while meeting or exceeding expectations. To solve a need you need to have a clearly defined and agreed upon problem then resolve the problem. Meeting or exceeding expectations requires you to ensure alignment on the project. Project alignment matches project expectations or goals and the ultimate project deliverables. It may sound easy but many people mess this up by not clearly understanding the project expectations. Ensuring proper project alignment requires you to ask three fundamental questions: what do you want; when do you want it; and how do you want it?

Answering the first question will let you know what the person assigning the project expects. You can receive further clarification by confirming what resources; processes or methodology such as templates, forms, databases, and the person assigning the project wants to see utilized.

The answer to the second question should help to confirm your deadline. No matter what date you're given, plan on completing the project early. Things will inevitably come up so don't fall victim to Murphy's Law—what can go wrong, will go wrong. If you're not given a deadline, suggest one when discussing this question and agree upon a deadline. Once agreed upon, prepare to deliver the project early in light of the deadline agreed upon.

The final question ensures that the anticipated final project deliverable meets the expectations of the project initiator, would they like your findings delivered by email, phone call, short or long memo, or some other specific form or template. If cost may be incurred, make sure you've agreed upon a budget and what the process is for any overages; for example, do you need approval, who do you need it from, etc.?

Your success on any project will be dramatically increased by asking these three questions and by complying with the responses. It's hard to be wrong if your delivery adheres to the responses – I'd argue it's almost impossible.

YOU ARE A BRAND, ACT LIKE IT

Entrepreneurship or knowing how to make money is good, but that doesn't mean that being employed is bad or something that you shouldn't aspire to achieve. You don't have to chose one at the exclusion of the other, instead take the core principles of entrepreneurship and apply them to your employment as if you are the product and your employer (or prospective employers) are the purchasers of the product (you). The same rules of sales apply.

In Tom Peters' landmark article "The Brand Called You" he encouraged professionals to focus on the feature-benefit that they offer. He described the feature benefits as the identifiable or distinguishable benefits that you offer to your employer. Examples of feature benefits that he suggested were your ability to deliver consistent work on time, or your ability to deliver dependable service that meets strategic needs for an internal or external customer. Do you complete projects under budget, anticipate or solve problems before they arise, or save money for your organization through your efficient ideas or work processes?

The key, as Peters described it, is to ask yourself: "What do I do that adds remarkable, measurable, distinguished, distinctive value? What do I do that I am most proud of? What have I accomplished that I can unabashedly brag about?" The process requires you to become relentlessly focused on how you add value to your projects and your organization.

Most people dislike personal branding because they feel that it shines the spotlight on themselves instead of on their colleagues or on their company. But this view incorrectly assigns success to only one person in the process and doesn't allow for anyone else to receive equal or more credit at the same time. It further assumes that your ambition is something negative to an organization. I disagree. To paraphrase a famous line from the movie Wall Street, "ambition is good."

Focusing on your brand generally causes you to focus on how to improve your company. While at first glance it may seem as though you're acting selfishly to grow and promote yourself, your company benefits from your increased performance and productivity and heightened focus on value generation. In addition you'll strive to provide beneficial leadership to the organization, and likely generate positive exposure and recognition from your personal branding activities. Most savvy companies will leverage your brand for recruiting purposes to demonstrate to recruits and prospects the type of talented individuals within the organization.

With your brand established and growing, it's time to promote it to ensure that others know about your product and what you have to offer; you have to gain exposure for yourself. This is where local networks and professional organizations can be of great assistance. People within or outside of your organization can't buy what you're offering if they don't know about your product, so tell them. It doesn't have to be pushy or a hard sell, start with the basics of simply letting others know who you are and what you do. Once people within and outside of your organization know who you are and what you do, you have to periodically remind them that you are out there and that you are willing to assist if they need the skills you have to offer. Whether the reminder is formally or informally communicated, the key is to remain diligent and consistent to ensure that the message is received.

I typically enjoy meeting with key stakeholders within and outside of my organization for coffee or lunch to share what I've been up to. I always spend significant time finding out what these individuals are up to as well. The general exchange of information usually works well to keep both of us informed about the exciting things that each person is working on. And more importantly, it helps to keep our respective skills top of mind with each other if and when the need arises for those skills.

Up to this point, if you have demonstrated great performance, projected the correct image and gained proper exposure, you should be well on your way to a management or leadership position within your organization. But even if you're not given a formal title, you can still show your leadership skills by being a connector.

CONNECT AND LEAD

People mistakenly think that you need a formal title to lead. However, leadership is merely a process where you use your influence on others to accomplish a common goal or objective. It doesn't require a specific title or rank. In fact there are many things that you can do that doesn't require a formal title to take a leadership role; like volunteering for internal projects, or assuming additional responsibility in your current role.

Don't make the mistake of thinking that you need to be a senior executive or have a high salary or executive perks before you can influence others. You can begin leading and influencing others right now if you practice actively assisting or inspiring others to achieve their goals. If you want to lead, help others to dream or set their vision, then help them to accomplish that vision by connecting them with those that make their dreams possible. Sound familiar? It should, it's the same principles we explored in Chapter 3 when we discussed mentoring. That's why mentors are so important; they're leaders without a title. As Henry Kissinger, the American political scientist, diplomat, and recipient of the Nobel Peace Prize said, "The task of the leader is to get his people from where they are to where they have not been." Be a leader and use your connections to assist people from getting where they are to where they'd like to be.

We've confirmed that leaders are connectors. They connect people with things they want or need. They concentrate a significant portion of their existence to finding out what those around them want or need, and then focus on helping those individuals acquire what they desire.

Why should you be a connector? It seems like a ton of work. Why would you spend a significant amount of time focused on helping others instead of focusing on how you can get ahead—aren't these principles supposed to be about *your* professional success not how to make *others* successful? That's a reasonable question to ask, but I need you to pay close attention, because my response may be the most important principle of all: *you can't be successful without focusing on the success of others.* The more you give, the more you'll receive. You can't expect to be helped if you're not helping others.

A connector is an information hub. They listen more than they speak. They are keenly interested in what you are doing, what you have done, and what you want to do, so they can help you accomplish your goals. Connectors match those with critical resources with those that need them. Because of this, they are highly sought after and deeply valued. People naturally gravitate to a connector because of what or who the connector may know, people want access to the information the connector has. And in return, when a connector needs assistance, there are usually a number of individuals willing to help because of the valuable assistance the connector has and will provide. The connector benefits because of their goodwill.

Think of connectors as a concierge of sorts. The best hotels in the world are those that have superb concierge service. If you need tickets to the hottest show or seats to the top restaurants they make it happen. The ability to connect people to what they seek is highly valuable—businesses and successful individuals know this. In the age we live in, information is the key to power and influence. One of the most successful businesses in the world, Google, was built on this principle—connecting people through their search engine to what they want, when they want it. And as you know, their ability to connect has made them extremely successful by any standard you can apply. Do the same in your professional relationships. Practice this skill of connecting others to their desires. Start listening more than you speak. Focus intently on what people desire and cross-reference it against the needs that you've observed for others. The more you can connect people, the more successful you'll become.

DREAM BIG BUT KNOW HOW TO PIVOT

Before we conclude this chapter, I want to encourage you to always permit yourself to dream big about what you can accomplish professionally, but allow your dreams the flexibility to change. Success is rarely accidental. You have to plan your work then work your plan. Develop a detailed plan outlining what you want and consider how you'll get it. If you don't get it that's ok, because you are working your plan.

Develop a one, three, and five-year plan with detailed steps and action items to help guide you along the way. But understand that it's just a guide; it helps you to reach your destination, but isn't the destination itself.

Eric Ries, a successful entrepreneur and advisor to many high growth companies coined the phrase "pivot" to define the concept of changing directions while still staying grounded in what you've learned. A pivot is typically associated with high-tech companies, and is a process used to develop or modify new products. However, it can apply to your professional development as well. As Mr. Ries has shown, a pivot allows you to stop focusing on unsuccessful things by building on what worked even as you learn from your failures. It allows you to be flexible while keeping your original vision.

When your vision fails, you can modify it, but it shouldn't be done at the first sign of trouble. Instead, you should obtain feedback to find out whether what you want to do is compatible with what you can do. Mentors, as we discussed in Chapter 3, are excellent resources to bounce such questions off of. They will provide you with honest feedback while suggesting ways to improve and build upon what you have learned about your vision so you can continue on your path to success. Don't abandon your dream by jumping from one vision to something completely different. Instead, learn from your past successes even if the ultimate result was a failure and use those specifics to continue to work your plan.

As you work your plan, ensure that you're developing relevant leadership and management experience that's consistent with your level of experience. Typically, your first five years should be spent doing or developing critical skills and strong tactical capabilities. The next five years usually begins your formal leadership development training. During this period you should have mastered the tactical skills required in your profession and may begin developing management and strategic thinking skills that benefit your organization.

The period of growth between years ten - fifteen should demonstrate your leadership and management capabilities through consistently generated results. This period generally requires you to demonstrate an ability to lead people and projects in a manner that generates revenue or reduces expenses for your organization. With fifteen or more years of experience you are usually expected to possess strong management and leadership experience.

The results obtained during this period should increase and scale in correlation to the larger number of people or projects that you now manage.

As you progress, it is assumed that you have mastered the skills at the previous level. Through each phase, ensure that the skills, experiences and relationships you've developed demonstrate your preparedness for promotion to the next level within your organization.

Finally, although we've discussed several principles that should make you extremely successful as a professional, not every opportunity will be seem positive or beneficial to you or your career at the outset, but you've got to train yourself to find and focus on the positive. When life gives you lemons, don't make lemonade; make champagne. Make the most out of bad professional situations.

For example, if you're given a large review project that's tedious or boring, use the experience to build time management or project management skills, or demonstrate your ability to complete or implement the assignment on time and on budget.

Don't allow an initial challenge to frustrate your purpose and cause you to quit. Studies have shown that the only thing that separates successful people from unsuccessful persons is that successful people don't quit; they don't give up on their dreams. They may modify their vision but they don't give up their dreams of success. They don't give up because they know that if they keep trying, eventually they'll succeed. Unsuccessful people, however, will give up before they have truly started their journey; proving the saying, you are not guaranteed to succeed if you try, but you are guaranteed to fail if you don't!

Apply the pivot method to your career by becoming determined to accomplish your goal, and follow through until you achieve it, even if it means modifying the original vision or some of the steps you thought you'd take. Ask yourself with each failure, "What can I learn from this?" Then take the answer and build upon it until you reach your professional goals.

CHAPTER 6: FINANCIAL PRINCIPLES

It's not what you start with,
but what you do with what you've been given

So you've spoken to the future you, received a great education, built your brand and are now a successful professional. Although you've worked hard to unlock your earning potential, you'll have to work even harder to ensure that your money works diligently for you long after you've achieved success.

As we saw in Chapter 5 having a plan is critical. While it's important to have a plan for your career, you also have to have a plan for your money. Proper financial planning will allow your financial decisions to support your professional goals, and provide you with financial security. You don't need a large income to begin planning; you can start with the money you are earning now. What's most important is understanding how to create, increase and preserve wealth—not income; many people mistakenly use the terms interchangeably.

Generally speaking, wealth is excess beyond your needs. Income, however, is generally defined as wages received. Thus, wealth is accumulated from excess income. You can be wealthy without a large income, but a large income doesn't necessarily mean that you are wealthy. Therefore, the lower your personal expenses, the more income you will have available to generate wealth.

Don't let appearances fool you. Individuals with larger than average incomes may live a wealthy lifestyle with lavish homes, cars and vacations, among other things; but they may not be wealthy. They could be living paycheck to paycheck. Conversely, the person who seems to be poor because she lives modestly and has a frugal lifestyle of discount shopping and coupon clipping may have significant wealth because she lives within her means. The frugal individual likely has a substantial balance in her savings account for emergencies, with significant funds set aside for retirement, in addition to being able to purchase items she desires with cash instead of borrowing on a credit card.

Countless research has concluded that wealth begets wealth, and the lack of wealth perpetuates the same. Recently, a study conducted by Thomas Shapiro following a large number of the same families between 1984 and 2007 found that families who lack wealth typically have less money to pay for college, less money to invest in a business, and less money for emergencies. Such a gap, Mr. Shapiro noted, denies and assures economic inequality for the next generation.

Research has also confirmed that wealth is power. It empowers you to choose your environment and generally your experience of life. It also provides you with liberty, or the freedom to choose, and the ability to pursue happiness as you define it.

We live in the freest society on earth, but many are slaves to debt. Many people don't realize this and mistakenly think they are free since they are not oppressed by a governmental entity. You may be oppressed, however, if you don't have the freedom to choose. Choice depends on the freedom to choose. If you're shackled with debt you don't have the freedom to choose.

In many cases, individuals in debt—those without wealth—lack the freedom to choose. They can't take advantage of various opportunities because they're too busy trying to make ends meet so they miss opportunities; or they don't have the financial wherewithal to seize those opportunities when they arise. For example, you'd like to live in a better neighborhood, drive a more reliable car, or send your child to a better school, but you can't do any of these things because you can't afford it. Unfortunately, in each of these scenarios you can't choose the more desirable alternative because you don't have enough excess income available.

Let's take a moment to explore how you can accumulate enough wealth to give you the freedom to choose the life you want to live.

HOW TO ACCUMULATE WEALTH

You can begin accumulating wealth with any income received. Whether it's received from a paper route, flipping burgers, doing social work or performing surgery; you simply have to follow the Platinum and Gold rules of money management. The Platinum rule requires you to save a portion of what you make by living beneath your means. The Golden rule directs you to purchase assets— or items with an established market that increase in value over time, instead of liabilities—or items that decrease in value over time and/or require additional outlays of cash to continue to own. Follow the Platinum and Gold rules and you'll be well on your way to accumulating substantial wealth.

Even though these rules are simple, it's easy to confuse an asset with a liability, especially if you've paid a lot of money for an item. The mistake occurs when you believe that someone else will be willing to pay more for the same item simply because you paid a large amount for the item. This logic is what investors call "speculation." Such thinking lacks any evidence to support the assumption that there's a market of buyers willing to pay more for the item. And therefore increases the likelihood that the anticipated increased future value will never occur, since you'll likely never be able to sell the item. If you do, it will sell for less than what you paid.

Compare such speculative behavior against what intelligent investors like Warren Buffet do; they only purchase assets after thorough analysis demonstrates with reasonable certainty that the asset will maintain its original purchase price and increase in value over time. This approach has made countless individuals wealthy, including Buffet, who is one of the wealthiest individuals alive and arguably one of the greatest investors who has ever lived. If it works for them, it will work for you too: buy assets, not liabilities or speculative items.

Despite the reliability the Platinum and Golden rules provide for generating wealth, some still believe that wealth is only acquired through inheritance, not by saving and spending wisely. According to a 2010 study by the Spectrem Group, most wealth isn't inherited it's earned. The study showed that wealth usually results from investing, savings accumulated by living beneath your means and being frugal, hard work, and taking calculated and well-informed professional and financial risks.

The Spectrem Group study also disproved the popular belief that only doctors, lawyers, actors and athletes can accumulate substantial wealth through their jobs. Although those tend to be the typical professions highlighted by the media when showcasing wealthy individuals, the study affirmed that 90% of those who create significant wealth of more than one million dollars are college graduates; but less than 8% of those individuals also have a law or medical degree.

It's clear that saving and spending wisely are excellent ways to accumulate wealth, but there are a host of simple strategies you can employ to maximize your wealth.

STRATEGIES TO MAXIMIZE YOUR WEALTH

A recent article in Money Magazine by Paul J. Lim and George Mannes highlighted how easy it is to generate significant wealth. The key the authors suggested is to maximize three critical factors: the time you have to work with; how much you save; and how you invest your savings. According to the authors, it's not fatal if you can't save as much or invest as well as you'd like to, so long as you save and invest longer—as the Rolling Stones famously sang, time is on your side! The article concludes that you're far better off being a consistent saver who's a mediocre investor than being a below-average saver who beats the stock market.

Being a consistent saver requires discipline to budget and save. Consistent savers typically develop, maintain and monitor a personal budget that tracks their discretionary spending. Most individuals don't like to budget or fail to do it consistently because it's either too hard to keep track of the information being tracked, or because they simply don't want to know or deal with their financial situation. However, creating, maintaining and monitoring a budget doesn't have to be difficult, scary or time consuming.

One of the easiest budgeting methods is to track only your disposable income, not your fixed or recurring costs that are identical, or almost identical like groceries and toiletries, each month like housing, utilities and major loans like your auto, home, and educational loans. Your budget would then account for how much disposable income, or income that's not tied to a specific expense,

you have for that pay period and you'll have the freedom
to decide if or how you want to spend that free cash.

For example, if you make $2,000 every two weeks after
taxes and your fixed costs are $1,500 every two weeks,
you'd create a budget for that two-week period of $500
and decide how you'll spend and save that amount until
your next paycheck. You may set aside $200 for savings;
spend $150 on entertainment and dining out, $100 on gas
and $50 on gifts and personal hobbies.

Your budget doesn't have to be perfect at first; it can
be adjusted and refined over time. It's only critical that
you start and monitor your progress so you can start
to accumulate wealth now. Your budget is part of your
financial plan, and as with all planning, it will require you
to be flexible so that you can adjust and pivot if you don't
hit the goals you've set for yourself.

You may find in the first couple months of budgeting
that you don't have disposable income to cover your fixed
costs. If that's the case, you need to make the sometimes-
difficult decision to reconsider what items are critical and
see if you can eliminate those expenses at least temporarily
until your budget allows for those expenses. For example,
you may have to sell a vehicle, get a roommate or move to
less expensive housing, or significantly reduce or eliminate
your dining out or entertainment spending.

In addition to budgeting, there are several things that most financial experts suggest to maximize your wealth:

- Pay yourself first by setting aside ideally 10% of your income, if possible.

- Live beneath your means by saving raises and living on last year's income.

- "Set and forget" your savings by setting up an automatic savings account with your bank.

- Surround yourself like-minded savers to avoid keeping up with the Joneses. Seek out people who save and spend wisely and associate with them if you have common interests.

- Shop and consume strategically by comparison shopping, using coupons or by using Internet deal sites like Groupon or Living Social, and wait for sales. More importantly, once purchased, use items in full before they expire to ensure you are getting the most out of the item.

- Generate additional income by getting a second job, selling the stuff that you don't need. If all else fails, ask for a raise if you consistently add value to your organization and haven't received an increase in more than a year.

- Respect debt by only buying what you can afford, avoid carrying consumer credit balances of more than 30 days, know your credit score and periodically check it for errors. This should allow you to generate a high FICO credit score that shows you're responsible to lenders and can qualify you for favorable rates on home and auto loans, and insurance coverage. Some employers may also include credit checks as part of the hiring process as an indication of your responsibleness, so maintaining a high credit score may positively impact your employment opportunities as well.

- Max out your 401(k) match; most employers offer a match so take advantage of the free money.

- Use tax-advantaged accounts like 401(k) s and IRAs that allow you to build wealth faster by permitting the money to grow tax deferred.

All of these tips will be useless if you don't put them into action and make them part of who you are. The principle of saving more than you earn has to be cooler to you than spending above your means is. Begin measuring your worth by what you build, with your family, in your community, at your company, not by what you buy.

SAVING HAS TO BE COOL

It's easier to accumulate wealth if you've convinced yourself that saving money is better, more hip, or trendier than buying the newest gadget, gizmo, or accessory. Be brutally honest with yourself regarding your financial situation and force yourself to see the alternatives.

For example, you probably don't *need* a new car; instead, you may be able to throw some new tires on your current ride or do other maintenance to spruce it up. Similarly, you may not need a new computer simply because your hard drive is getting slow; perhaps you can get an external hard drive and store files there, or you can remove old files and keep using it as-is. Recognize "wants" versus "needs" and prioritize accordingly, then find sensible alternatives to address your wants. Remember, it's not what you start with, but what you do with what you have been given that matters.

Many people dream of making millions, but don't realize that they're on that path already. Start thinking of your income as lottery installments. Assuming you're generating $50,000 per year in income, you'll make a million dollars in approximately 20 years. When you look at your income that way, what will you have to show for the money you've made? What will you do with it? Will it be used wisely? Hopefully you will be a good steward and use it in ways that are beneficial to you and your family now, and well into the future. Instead of tragically squandering your financial resources on things you don't need to impress people you don't like.

CHAPTER 7: FINDING AND CREATING TRUE WORK-LIFE BALANCE

Don't get so busy making a living that you forget to make a life

The problem with striving to be successful is that once you attain your goal it can consume other parts of your life, so you have to be disciplined to ensure that you don't let work become the end-all-be-all of your existence. Work is a means to an end; it's a tool to provide you with income for other things. Don't work so much that you can't find time to do, or are too exhausted to do other things.

The current President of Israel, Shimon Peres, said that a person's purpose in life is, "to find a cause that's larger than yourself and then to give your life to it." There's never been a single dying person who regretted not working more as they took their final breath. No one; my dad sure didn't. Instead, you typically wish that you spent more time doing what you love, creating memories.

Time is too precious a commodity to spend it on things that aren't valuable to you. You can't get it back, so manage it wisely. Create the work-life balance you desire. Stop spending time complaining or blaming others and do what all successful individuals do—plan and execute a successful strategy to gain more time for other pursuits outside of work. Define what's important to you outside of work and commit to investing more time in those people or activities. If you don't make these choices for yourself, someone else will and you will likely not be happy with the result!

The Mayo Clinic studied the affects of failing to pursue other interests outside of work, and concluded that it can lead to serious health problems such as the inability to think clearly and work productively due to fatigue; as well as high-blood pressure, hypertension and increased risks of a stroke due to high-levels of stress. It also can lead to poor eating habits and lack of exercise; and cause mild to severe levels of depression from not spending quality time with friends and loved ones.

STRATEGIES TO IMPROVE WORK-LIFE BALANCE

Balancing the increased expectations and responsibilities that come from being a successful professional with the demands of your personal life will likely continue to be an ongoing challenge. However, given the severe health risks, you can deal with the challenges by employing many of the following strategies to improve your work-life balance:

- Perform an audit of your career and personal life to identify critical items that warrant your focus and time. Eliminate or delegate things that aren't as important to you so you can focus on the things that are.

- Protect your time and learn to say "no." Most people respond to requests for their time, even when they don't have it to give, because they either enjoy the activity or they don't want to disappoint the person asking. Saying "yes" to these things creates stress when you spread yourself thin. Saying no upfront in a pleasant way allows you to maintain strong relationships while decreasing the strain you'll have on your mind and or body due to another meaningless activity.

- Take what you've got. Does your employer have flexible work options? If so, take advantage of those benefits. Shorter work weeks, telecommuting, sabbaticals or other flexible scheduling options allow you to reduce your stress through the increased control you'll have over your work schedule.

- TAKE YOUR VACATION! It's yours, you've earned it, and it helps you to physically and mentally recover from a hectic work schedule. It also reduces diminished productivity that occurs due to fatigue.

- Manage your time at work better. You often have to stay later at work because you've spent more time than you should have participating in hallway conversations about non-work activities, surfing the web, or making personal calls. None of these activities by themselves are inappropriate if you're doing it to de-stress on a particularly stressful day or from a stressful project. However, if you're finding that you're constantly staying late because of such ineffective use of your time, you may want to consider cutting many of these breaks since they seem to lead to more stressful situations—longer hours in the office.

- Plan your play, including volunteering and exercise, and don't allow it to get postponed. Apply the same level of intensity and focus that you use at work, when you have fun outside of work. Proactively schedule these events and don't let them get interrupted, just like you don't allow your scheduled meetings and appointments at work to be interrupted by non-work activities.

- Eat healthy and exercise. Research shows that healthy eating and exercise increases your energy level and helps you to concentrate on mentally challenging tasks. It's difficult to find the time to exercise, but if you're creative, you can find a way to pack 30 minutes of activity into your daily activities. For example, park in the farthest spot in the parking lot to increase your time spent walking. Take the stairs instead of the elevator. Walk around the block every few hours to get your heart rate up. Take calls standing up or moving around your office. All of these activities can be done quickly and with little effort to get you in the habit of staying active.

- Do little things to recharge your batteries like watch a movie, read your favorite magazines, go for a walk in your neighborhood, or listen to music.

Whatever you do, find time to pursue other interests outside of work, your mind and your body will thank you for it.

DON'T STRANGLE THE GOLDEN GOOSE

Although it's important to have a healthy balance between work and your personal life, it is critical that you don't go to extremes trying to live your life. Relax and have fun when appropriate, but always maintain a sense of priority for your job. Not necessarily a top priority, but definitely near the top of your list, below faith, family and fun.

It's easy to let leisure activities sidetrack you or take away your time and mental focus from your primary responsibilities—don't. Maintain a balance that allows you to excel at work and at play, without sacrificing one for the other. Whenever possible, limit extended leisure activities to non-work hours if they're not business related or associated with your scheduled vacation or time off. This ensures that your leisure activities won't jeopardize your employment, and create the added stress of losing and having to find a job.

Verify that any volunteer or secondary activities like boards, external committees or projects won't distract from what you do at work before agreeing to participate. Make sure your company supports the activity and doesn't view it as a distraction. If so, find ways to gain support by demonstrating to your company how it benefits what you do in your current role. For example, does it build new skills, allow you to network, or increase visibility for your company? If so, let your employer know.

Try to find ways to make volunteer or secondary activities beneficial for your company as well as yourself.

Consider whether you can get more business for the company, or introduce key external stakeholders to your internal stakeholders. There are always opportunities to find a mutually beneficial solution for you and your organization—take the time to look for them.

No matter how busy you become because of your profession, you have to make time for interests outside of work to maintain a proper work-life balance. Failure to do so could cause you to find yourself stressed, lonely, unhealthy, or even out of a job.

CONCLUSION

You're not guaranteed to succeed if you try, but you're guaranteed to fail if you don't

Well, here we are, at the end; or is it? You have explored all of the principles so you should know by now that you are far from concluding your journey. In fact, this is just the beginning. It's time for you to implement the principles we have explored, if you haven't begun doing so already.

It's time for you to achieve professional and financial success, without having to sacrifice time spent with your family or having it detract from your leisure activities. You know the secrets; you've learned the principles that can change your life forever; now you can begin living the life you want!

The thought of doing this may be scary. I know because I've been there. Now is when the doubt begins to creep in and you begin to wonder if you can really do it. You can. You owe it to yourself to try. You may be thinking, "what if it doesn't work?" Consider instead, *what if it does?* How will your life be different after you've achieved personal, professional and financial success? What can you do, who can you help, and what legacy can you leave for your family, your friends and your community?

Take the first step and find out. Commit to find a mentor in the next week to help you on your journey. Pick a person, or more if necessary, that you know, admire and trust and utilize their knowledge, wisdom and experience to help guide you on your path to success. If you get lost, I'll be here, waiting in these pages to remind you of the principles you've learned. You can revisit them anytime and in any order you want to refresh your memory—that's the benefit of written advice.

And even though you'll be seeking a mentor, don't overlook your ability to mentor someone else. You have the knowledge, wisdom and experience that you can share with someone who has yet to explore the path you have traveled. Help them to get from where they are to where they are going by sharing your story. It costs you nothing but may gain you everything—the unbridled joy of yielding success in the life of another person.

Before I go, I'd like to thank you for allowing me the opportunity to travel with you on this leg of your journey.

It's been an honor and a privilege that I don't take lightly.
I hope you continue to press toward the mark of success,
and that when you arrive you experience all that you
desire.

I look forward to seeing you on the path.

Warmest regards,
Al

POSTSCRIPT: TAKE THE PLEDGE

Find a Sage | Be a Sage

Hopefully, our time together has convinced you that mentors are important. This isn't a new revelation; many cultures have recognized this fact. Whether called a teacher, wise man, philosopher, rabbi, priest, or guru, the concept was the same. Younger generations would seek the advice, wisdom and counsel of the wise older person. And the older person, in return, would gladly impart their knowledge and wisdom with those that respectfully sought it, and continue to guide the younger person on their path to success.

In many ancient cultures this profoundly wise person was called a Sage. The first step on your path to success is to find a Sage. Once successful, it's critical that you be a Sage; and help others along their path to success. That's the essence of the principles explored. If you retain nothing else from our time together, remember this:

Find a Sage, Be a Sage.

Make that your mantra and you'll be well on your way to personal, professional and financial success.

Confirm your commitment to these principles by taking the Sage Pledge. It costs you nothing, can be done immediately and privately, and doesn't need to be performed in any specific way. Simply declare your desire to invest in yourself and others by Finding a Sage and Being a Sage.

SAGE PLEDGE

As a Mentee, I acknowledge that it's wise to learn from other and I commit to:

- Invest in my personal, professional and financi development by seeking the wisdom of other wis individuals;

- Respect the time invested in me by applying the wisdo obtained when applicable, and share the results wit those that provided the insight; and

- Repay the investment made in me by investing in othe whenever I have knowledge or wisdom to share

As a Mentor, I acknowledge that I have knowledge and wisdo that others may benefit from and I commit to:

- Share my knowledge and wisdom with those in need; and

- Invest in the success of at least one individual by sharing my knowledge, wisdom and personal network with this individual to enhance their position and visibility, and continue to invest until the person achieves their goal.

By:_____ Date:_____

ADDITIONAL RESOURCES

The following resources provided tremendous guidance in my pursuit of personal, professional and financial success:

Books:

The Purpose Driven Life (Zondervan, 2002) by Rick Warren
The Jesus I Never Knew (Zondervan, 2002) by Phillip Yancey
What Jesus Meant (Penguin, 2007) by Garry Wills
Mere Christianity (HarperSanFrancisco, 2001) by C.S. Lewis
Rich Dad, Poor Dad (Warner Books, 2002) by Robert T. Kiyosaki
The Total Money Makeover (Thomas Nelson, 2009) by Dave Ramsey
The Millionaire Next Door (Pocket, 1998) by Thomas J. Stanley and William D. Danko
Good to Great (Collins, 2001) by Jim Collins
The Mis-education of the Negro (Createspace, 2011 Reprint) by Carter G. Woodson
"How To Steal Like An Artist" (March 30, 2011 Blog post) by Austin Kleon
"A Brief Guide to World Domination" (June 24, 2008 Self-published PDF) by Chris Guillebeau

Blogs/Magazines:

Frugal Dad | frugaldad.com
Gather Little by Little | gatherlittlebylittle.com
Get Rich Slowly | getrichslowly.org/blog
Will Teach You to Be Rich | iwillteachyoutoberich.com
The Simple Dollar | thesimpledollar.com

Evil HR Lady | *evilhrlady.blogspot.com*
HBR.org *(Harvard Business Review)*
Knowledge@Wharton | *knowledge.wharton.upenn.edu*
McKinsey Quarterly | *mckinseyquarterly.com*
Penelope Trunk | *blog.penelopetrunk.com*
Success Magazine blog | *blog.success.com*
BBC News | *bbc.co.uk/news*
Business Insider | *businessinsider.com*
The Economist | *economist.com*
Fast Company | *fastcompany.com*
Fortune | *money.cnn.com/magazines/fortune*
The New York Times | *nytimes.com*
The Wall Street Journal | *online.wsj.com*

In addition, I want to give special recognition to the blogs of the following individuals; they provided invaluable insight into the development, marketing and production of this book: Joel Konrath, Justine Musk, Joanna Penn, Alan Rinzler, Chris Guillebeau and the Publetariat blog. Thank you dearly for generously sharing your knowledge and wisdom with us all.

REFERENCES

The following sources were used to develop some of the concepts explored in this book:

Labor Force Characteristics by Race and Ethnicity, 2009, U.S. Department of Labor, U.S. Bureau of Labor Statistics, August 2010.

National Populations Projections Press Release, August 14, 2008; U.S. Census Bureau.

"Is Your Job an Endangered Species?" by Andy Kessler, February 17, 2011; *The Wall Street Journal.*

Benefits of Mentoring, A Booklet by Triple Creek Associates; http://www.3creek.com

"Quick Facts about Student Debt" (Updated January 2010); The Project on Student Debt.

"Average Starting Salary to Class of 2011 Up 3.5 Percent," (NACE *Spring 2011 Salary Survey* report), February 10, 2011; National Association of Colleges and Employers.

"30 Ways to Reduce College Costs", Student Aid on the Web; U.S. Department of Education.

"Simon Sinek: How Great Leaders Inspire Action", Filmed September 2009, TED.com

Small Giants: Companies that Choose to be Great Instead of Big (Portfolio, 2005), Bo Burlingham.

Empowering Yourself: The Organizational Game Revealed (AuthorHouse, 2010), Harvey J. Coleman.

The Cambridge Handbook of Expertise and Expert Performance (Cambridge Handbooks in Psychology) (Cambridge University Press, 2006); K. Anders Ericsson, Neil Charness, Paul J. Feltovich and Robert R. Hoffman.

Outliers: The Story of Success (Back Bay Books, 2011 Reprint); Malcolm Gladwell.

"The Brand Called You" by Tom Peters, August 31, 1997; *Fast Company Magazine.*

"Pivot, don't jump to a new vision" by Eric Ries, June 22, 2009; *Lessons Learned blog.*

"The Racial Wealth Gap Increases Four Fold" by Thomas M. Shapiro, Tatjan Meschede, and Laura Sullivan; Institute on Assets and Social Policy Research and Policy Brief May 2010.

"Meet the Millionaires" 8 Page Interactive Slideshow by Money Magazine staff; money.cnn.com

"How to become a millionaire in 3 easy steps" by Paul J. Lim and George Mannes, April 5, 2011; money.cnn.com.

"Work-life balance: Tips to reclaim control" by Mayo Clinic staff; mayoclinic.com.

ABOUT THE AUTHOR

Coleman is a highly-awarded lawyer, professor and writer living
ar St. Paul, Minnesota with his wife and three beautiful children.
devoted mentor to a multitude of exceptional emerging leaders
business, law, government, non-profits, the arts and science
roughout the country. He wrote *Secrets to Success: The Definitive*

Career Development Guide for New and First Generation Professionals to candidly share principles of personal, professional and financial success with tomorrow's leaders.

In his current role as Director and Senior Corporate Counsel at a leading U.S. tax and business consulting firm, Al advises, manages or supports a full range of business and legal issues including complex commercial transactions and corporate strategy, advertising and marketing review and approval, intellectual property development and portfolio management, mergers and acquisitions, and resolution of complex commercial disputes.

To relax, Al enjoys traveling, cooking, golfing and spending time with friends and family—or any combination of these activities.

His bio can be found on LinkedIn at:
linkedin.com/in/alcolemanjr

Follow him on Twitter @alcolemanjr

Read more of his thoughts on the Secrets to Success at:
alcolemanjr.com

Discuss the Secrets to Success with others at:
www.facebook.com/alcolemanjr

And share stories of your success with him at:
alcolemanjr@gmail.com

15.19

CPSIA information can be obtained at www.ICGtesting.com
Printed in the USA
LVOW120456211011

251489LV00003B/26/P